MW00438673

EXPLAINING
Being Anointed and Filled
with the Holy Spirit

DAVID PAWSON

ANCHOR RECORDINGS

First published in Great Britain in 2016 by
Anchor Recordings Ltd
Synegis House, 21 Crockhamwell Road,
Woodley, Reading RG5 3LE

**For more of David Pawson's teaching,
including DVDs and CDs, go to
www.davidpawson.com**

**FOR FREE DOWNLOADS
www.davidpawson.org**

**For further information,
email: info@davidpawsonministry.com**

ISBN 978-1-911173-18-2

Printed by Lightning Source

This booklet is based on a talk. Originating as it does from the spoken word, its style will be found by many readers to be somewhat different from my usual written style. It is hoped that this will not detract from the substance of the biblical teaching found here.

As always, I ask the reader to compare everything I say or write with what is written in the Bible and, if at any point a conflict is found, always to rely upon the clear teaching of scripture.

David Pawson

EXPLAINING
Being Anointed and Filled with the Holy Spirit

Let us look at three readings from the Word of God. Firstly, from John 1:

> The next day, John saw Jesus coming towards him and said, "Look, the Lamb of God, who takes away the sin of the world! This is the one I meant when I said, 'A man who comes after me has surpassed me because he was before me. I myself did not know him, but the reason I came baptising with water was that he might be revealed to Israel."
>
> Then John gave this testimony: "I saw the Spirit come down from heaven as a dove and remain on him. I would not have known him, except that the one who sent me to baptise with water told me, 'The man on whom you see the Spirit come down and remain is he who will baptise with the Holy Spirit.' I have seen and I testify that this is the Son of God." (John 1:29–34, NIV)

Two things you need: have your sins taken away by the Lamb of God and be baptised in the Holy Spirit. Both are needed to be a proper Christian. Let us now turn to Acts 19.

> While Apollos was at Corinth, Paul took the road through the interior and arrived at Ephesus. There he found some

disciples and asked them, "Did you receive the Holy Spirit when you believed?"

They answered "No, we have not even heard that there is a Holy Spirit."

So Paul asked, "Then what baptism did you receive?"

"John's baptism," they replied.

Paul said, "John's baptism was a baptism of repentance. He told the people to believe in the one coming after him, that is, in Jesus." On hearing this, they were baptised into the name of the Lord Jesus. When Paul placed his hands on them, the Holy Spirit came on them, and they spoke in tongues and prophesied. There were about twelve men in all. (Acts 19:1–7, NIV)

Did you notice that it wasn't just enough to believe? They needed to receive the Holy Spirit.

Finally, from the little letter to Titus:

At one time we too were foolish, disobedient, deceived and enslaved by all kinds of passions and pleasures. We lived in malice and envy, being hated and hating one another. But when the kindness and love of God our Saviour appeared, he saved us, not because of righteous things we had done, but because of his mercy. He saved us through the washing of rebirth and renewal by the Holy Spirit, whom he poured out on us generously [*the word is 'copiously'*] through Jesus Christ our Saviour, so that, having been justified by his grace, we might become heirs having the hope of eternal life. This is a trustworthy saying. And I want you to stress these things, so that those who have trusted in God may be careful to devote themselves to doing what is good. These things are excellent and profitable for everyone. (Titus 3:3–8, NIV)

Once again, there is a combination of two things – forgiveness and receiving the Holy Spirit. That is my theme.

Now I don't know if you know that in your Bible, in the New Testament, there are two baptists. Did you know that baptists went as far back as the Bible? You have heard of one – John the Baptist, but I wonder whether you have ever heard of the other? It was his cousin: Jesus the baptist. They are both given the same title. Both John and his cousin Jesus are called 'the baptist' in your New Testament. John became a baptist about four years before his cousin Jesus. Actually, the word is not a noun, it is literally 'John the baptiser' and 'Jesus the baptiser'. The New Testament never talks about *the* baptism of the Spirit, it talks about *being baptised* – always verbal, and the verb is something dynamic and moving. A noun is something static and fixed so John was the baptiser and Jesus was also called the baptiser. It was a nickname, not a name. It was not a nickname about what either of them *was*, but about what both of them *did*. That is why it is a verb.

What does the word 'baptise' mean?

So, the first thing I want to teach you is what the word *baptise* means. It is never translated into the English language. Your Bible simply has the Greek word transliterated which means not translated but simply spelled in English letters. Did you know that the deeds of a Bible publisher in England did not allow translating the Greek word 'baptise'? You can only render it in the Greek fashion. It is like 'rendezvous' in French. That is a French word meaning 'meet you' but we still use the French word transliterated into English letters.

So what does *baptise* – the Greek word – actually mean? In very simple terms, it means to put a solid into a liquid and of course we do that every day. If you have a bath, you are putting a solid into a liquid. In the Greek language they use it of things like this: a ship that sinks at sea is said to be baptised; a solid has been put into a liquid. Now when we hear of a ship being baptised we think of the Queen breaking a bottle of champagne over her bows and saying, 'May God bless all who sail in her.' But the Greeks use it only when a ship is sunk. Do you remember when the Coronia went down in the Bay of Biscay a few years back? Greek headlines in the newspapers: 'Coronia baptised' – sunk. They use the word when they dye wool in a colour dye and you have to make sure that every bit of the wool goes under, into the dye: you baptised wool to make it a different colour. You use it when you have a party. There will be a huge bowl of fruit punch or something a bit stronger, and each person is given a cup and they take the cup and put it in the liquid and bring it up full. They are said to baptise the cup.

If you went to a Greek Orthodox Church, even today, you would find that when they baptise a baby they push it three times right under the water. They have to have a font that big. If you go to some old parish churches in England you will see a big font that big – so that the baby can be baptised! A solid is put right in a liquid. A Greek church could never moisten a forehead and call that baptism because it means immersion; it means to be soaked, to be saturated through and through. It is a wonderful word and that is why they called John 'the baptiser'. It was a nickname and means John the dipper or John the Plunger or John the Immerser. That is what the word means! It was purely to defend moistening the forehead that you could not translate the word into English. In some languages, the word is translated into something like dip or plunge or sink or soak or saturate – a solid right inside a liquid.

Now that has got that word out of the way. Of course, John the Baptist we are told did this at a certain point on the River Jordan. When you go to see the Jordan you get a shock. It is what we would call a stream – a little river; and it is a dirty river. You think: how on earth did John the baptiser, John the dipper use this? But at a certain point in the river there is a deep pool. You know how rivers sometimes slow down and make a deep pool, and we are told in John 3 (you know v. 16, but I wonder if you know this verse in chapter 3) that John was baptising at Aenon near Salim because there was much water there. Nothing could be plainer.

In Acts 8, the Ethiopian eunuch, when he was baptised, said to Philip: 'See here is water, what hinders me to be baptised?' – and it says they *both went down into* the water. It is very clear that baptise means one thing and one thing only – to be put right into a liquid, soaked, saturated, covered completely.

John immersed in water because he had a special job to do. He had been told that the King is coming, the Kingdom is very near, and they had been waiting four hundred years and more for this – indeed a thousand years, because a thousand years earlier the Jews had been promised a king, the son of David who would bring the kingdom to Israel. They had waited a thousand years, but four hundred years previously God stopped talking to them and they didn't have a prophet for four hundred years, and each generation told their children that one day the king would come, and before he gets here there will be a prophet to tell us he is on his way. Having waited so long, no wonder when the prophet John the baptiser came, the whole nation went out. Here was a man from God saying that the king is coming, the kingdom is coming; get your life cleaned up.

You see, if you knew that Her Majesty The Queen was coming to visit your house, what would you do? I will guarantee the first thing the wives would do is to tell their husbands to get the vacuum cleaner out – to clean the place up as royalty is going to visit. If the Queen were coming to a service in your church, you would be having everything spick and span – you would really get red the carpet out, wouldn't you? And John's message was that the King is coming – get cleaned up. But he didn't say to get their houses cleaned up, he said to get the inside cleaned up. The King was coming and he was going to clean the situation up when he came; better for the people to clean up now than have him say: 'Look at your dirty life.'

Baptism is a Sacrament

So *he baptised to get people cleaned up* and he baptised in that dirty river. You think, when you see it, how can people get cleaned up in that? But it was what we call a sacrament. The Bible doesn't call it that, I am calling it that because a sacrament is a physical event with a spiritual effect. Baptism is a sacrament. It does something to you that is not physical. As Peter wrote in his letter, we are baptised not to clean our bodies up but to get a *clean conscience*. That is what baptism does for you. It gives you a clean conscience and you can only get a clean conscience if you have dealt with the dirt first. That is why John the Baptist said that there are conditions for being baptised in water. The first is that you confess that you are dirty, that you say that you need cleaning up, and that you actually name the things that have made your life dirty. Confession is never general in scripture. It is never, 'I must have sinned because everybody does' – that kind of confession is worthless. Confession is: 'I have done this … I have thought that … I have felt the other.' It is naming sins, and he taught that the first thing you do is confess your sins before he baptises you. You must admit you are dirty. There is no point in having a bath until you have admitted that.

Secondly, he said *you must repent, which means **putting right** what can be put right*. It means ending wrong

10

relationships. The Pharisees came and wanted to be baptised. He said 'You! You want to be baptised? You're not even confessing your sins yet.' He said, 'Bring forth fruit worthy of repentance.' When they asked what he meant, he said if you have too many clothes, give some away; if you are cooking your financial books, get your finance straightened out. Very practical is repentance, isn't it? It is something you *do*, not something you weep tears over – that is regret or even remorse. Repentance is *putting right* what can be put right.

So they had to confess what was wrong, put right what could be put right, and then they were ready for a 'bath', to get a clean conscience. They were ready for forgiveness of sins. You are not ready for forgiveness of sin until you have repented and confessed. Then, the water worked. Baptism does not always work. There are certain conditions that are needed for it to be a *sacrament*, and John was promising – you repent, you confess, and when I plunge you into this water, God will use it to clean your inside and you will come up out of that water with a clean conscience.

Baptism deals with past sins
I have had many times when somebody I have baptised has done just that and come out of the water clean. In fact, I baptised Cliff Richard and he wrote in his autobiography later: 'David Pawson washed me, rinsed me, and hung me up to dry' – and he said, 'I never felt so clean in all my life.' That is what baptism is for. It is a bath for dirty people and a burial for dead people, for people whose old life is finished; people who have turned away from the lifestyle they had been living and are leaving it behind – that is now dead and gone. So we have a burial – and when you combine a bath and a burial, you have baptism. So that was John. But he knew perfectly well that his baptism was not a permanent cure. He could get people clean but he couldn't keep them clean. He

11

could deal with their past but not their future. The problem is: if you have your conscience clean and you have cleaned up your lifestyle, how are you going to keep that up? Won't you just get dirty again quickly afterwards? The answer is yes. Baptism deals only with your past and cleans up your past. It doesn't clean up your future. John recognised that. He could get people ready for the King of Righteousness to come, get them cleaned up from their past, but how do you keep them clean then?

You need to be baptised in the Holy Spirit to stay clean
John said, 'You need another baptism – from someone else', and he constantly told everybody he baptised in water that they would need two baptisms and: there is a man coming after me who can give you the other baptism that you need that will keep you clean, that will clean up your future as well as your past. You need to be baptised in *Holy* Spirit. Or, if you like, *Clean* Spirit. You possibly use spirit to dry clean your clothes. Well, you need Holy Spirit if you are going to stay clean, because you won't manage it yourself, that is for sure. Getting your past dealt with is only half way and of itself will not prevent your sinning.

I remember the first time I sinned after I was baptised in water. I was so disappointed. I thought: 'I was going to live a clean life and it hasn't worked.' I did not then realise that baptism in water deals only with your past. It does clean that up.

Start the Christian life with a good bath and feel clean. That is why Jesus told us to do it. He wasn't thinking, 'What can I do as a test of discipleship? I know! I'll see if they are willing to get soaking wet in front of everybody else.' That is not what it is all about. And too many people think it is just a testimony to other people. It is nothing of the kind. It is starting life clean; and he will use that water. That is why Ananias said to Paul, 'What are you waiting for? Rise and be baptised and have your sins washed away.' I believe baptism works. It does clean up the inside of people. That is what it is for – to give them a clean start in the Christian life. But it won't keep them clean. You need another baptism for that and John said he could not do it for them but *He* will!

At the time he first said it, he did not know who that person was going to be. He got a shock when his cousin Jesus said 'baptise me', because already everybody knew that Jesus was living a totally clean life, and John said that Jesus should be baptising him, which showed that John, although he had baptised hundreds of others, had never been baptised himself. He said that Jesus should be baptising him, but Jesus said 'No. It is right to do what is right.' And any Christian today who makes the excuse 'I don't need to be baptised in water' must face the fact that Jesus found it necessary for himself, not to get cleaned up but to be obedient to God. That leaves anybody else without a single excuse, doesn't it?

In the normal Christian birth in the New Testament (as I have explained in my book of that title), baptism in water normally precedes baptism in Spirit. God is entitled to make exceptions but that is the normal rule.

Now let us move on. John knew first that the King was coming, but I don't think he knew who it was, and he knew that somebody else would be a baptiser – though not in water but in Holy Spirit. What John did know was that God had said that when he saw the Holy Spirit come down from heaven and rest and remain on someone he baptised, that was the one who was going to bring the other baptism. And he said he had seen it happen. He not only saw the dove come down, but he heard a voice that people thought was like a thunderclap. When God speaks out loud, it is very loud and it sounds just like a thunder clap. But John could hear the words. The crowd said 'What a thunder', but John heard

13

the words, 'This is my beloved Son and I am very pleased.' God was so pleased that Jesus was baptised. How dare any of us displease God by not doing it?

John therefore said two things about Jesus. He said, 'This is the Lamb of God that will take away the sin of the world'; and, 'this is the one who can baptise you in the Holy Spirit.' The latter is at the beginning of every one of the four Gospels, and yet I have heard so many preachers talk about the Lamb that takes away the sin of the world but so few saying that he is the one who baptises in the Holy Spirit. Isn't that crazy? More than that, only in one of the Gospels is it said, 'He is the Lamb of God that takes away the sins of the world' but in all four, 'He is the one who baptises in Holy Spirit.' More than that, when John said 'He is the Lamb that takes away the sin of the world', he only said that once in a private conversation, whereas when he said, 'This is the one who baptises in the Spirit', he said it to everybody.

We need two things – forgiveness and holiness

Now what has gone wrong with the church that somehow has the balance all the other way, always talking about the Lamb of God taking away the sins of the world, and the Cross, but never talking about Jesus the baptist. I am trying to redress the balance now. You need two things to get to heaven: forgiveness and holiness – 'without holiness no-one will see the Lord.' If you weren't holy before you got to heaven, you would ruin it very quickly for yourself and everybody else as it is a holy place. Actually, I don't talk much about heaven, I speak about the new heaven and the new Earth, because that is where we are going to live, and anything that would pollute that new universe will not be allowed in. If you went to heaven as you are – if I went to heaven as I am – we would spoil it. You can come and worship just as you are but you can't go to heaven just as you are. If we went just as we are now, it wouldn't be heaven for any of us.

So we need those two things – forgiveness and holiness – the first is the work of the second person of the Trinity, Jesus; the other is the work of the third person, the Holy Spirit. You need both, which means in simple terms that to live the Christian life you need to receive two persons, the second and third persons of the Trinity. You need Jesus and you need the Holy Spirit, and it is clear from scripture that you can have one without the other. That is a very important point. You read Acts chapter 8 if you want to know. There were some people who had repented of their sins, believed in Jesus, been baptised in water, were full of joy – and yet it says that none of them had received the Holy Spirit, so Peter and John came down from Jerusalem to pray for them. It was unheard of that somebody believed in Jesus but had not received the Spirit – they must put the situation right immediately.

I have to say that there are thousands in our churches who have received Jesus but don't know how to receive the Holy Spirit – and that is only half of your salvation. It is only half of what it takes to be a Christian. Yes, you have invited Jesus into your life, you have trusted him to take your sins away, but you are going to need more. There is a third person and his work is absolutely essential to live the Christian life. You need two baptisms; you need two persons who will then make you like God himself in whose image you were first created.

Now then, Jesus did many wonderful things during his lifetime. He healed the sick, cast out demons, stilled the storm, fed five thousand with a few fish and loaves. He did amazing things but not once did he baptise anyone in the Spirit. Did you ever notice that? John had said he would baptise you in the Holy Spirit. I can't do that for you but he will, and he never did while he was on Earth. Never once! I wonder if people noticed that; if they asked him. It does say that he was constantly talking about being baptised in the Spirit – did you know that? He was always talking about it but he never did it… until the last night of his life before he died. He said: I am going to talk to you now about the Holy Spirit, another Comforter. It is not a very nice word. It speaks of hot water bottles and cotton wool to me. "Comforter" in scripture is the Greek word '*paracletos*' or paraclete which means simply 'stand beside' – a lovely word: I am going to send you someone else who will stand beside you. And he then said a very interesting thing. He has been *with* you but he will be *in* you. He has been alongside you already but he wants to be inside you, and that is a really big step! Now, the Holy Spirit had been alongside the twelve apostles – after all, they had gone out and healed the sick and cast out demons and they could not have done that in their own power. The Holy Spirit was beside them because Jesus was beside them and the Holy Spirit was in Jesus. But he said on that last night that the Holy Spirit wants to be *inside you*, not just beside you, but in you and me. When you have Christ you have the Holy Spirit beside you in Christ. But you need him *inside*. That is a big change.

Jesus gave the disciples a sign and a command
The twelve disciples did not have that yet, so he promised that on the night he died. Then on the first night of his resurrection when he came back to them, again he talked to them about the Holy Spirit and he gave them a sign and a command. Now I want you to know this – nothing happened then. He said here is the sign, and he blew on each of them. After he had blown, he gave them a command – an imperative command: receive the Holy Spirit! And nothing happened. There is no record of their receiving, and in fact, out of eleven apostles, one of them was missing that night. Thomas was missing. So did he miss out on something? No,

the other ten would tell him when he came back that they had been given a sign and a command. When Jesus blows on us we must receive. It was a rehearsal for something that would happen fifty days later. That's all it was. There is no record of anything happening at that point. He blew on them and then commanded them 'now receive'. Had they received then, he would have told them to receive first and then would have blown on them. But he didn't – he blew then he told them to receive, and they knew that the next time Jesus blew on them they must surrender and receive what he was giving them. Six weeks later, he left them and went back to his home in heaven. He told them to wait. 'You will be baptised in the Holy Spirit not many days from now.' And it was ten days. Ten days later, nine o'clock in the morning, they are all in the temple – not the upper room – in the house of God, praying – a very public place. One hundred and twenty of them including Mary the mother of Jesus. Did you ever hear a preacher tell you that she spoke in tongues? Well, she did. And his brothers, instead of teasing him about his 'messianic syndrome', were now there praying. The ten are there, and Thomas is there, and now they have elected another – Matthias – to replace Judas. They are all there.

And now, at last, they were baptised in the Holy Spirit by Jesus in heaven. He never did it while he was on Earth. He said, 'I have to go back before he can come.' I've got to be up there for this to happen down here, and Jesus could only do it after he went back to heaven. That is why I said he became a baptist four years or thereabouts after his cousin John. But Jesus was baptising in the Holy Spirit, and now it happened, and for the first time in human history a group of people were baptised in the Holy Spirit by Jesus back in heaven.

I am sure you know the story well enough for me not to have to go through it, but there was an outside of it and an inside. The outside was wind blowing and fire sitting on each of them. Now that never happened again in the New Testament so far as we know. It has happened since. I was in a meeting of about a hundred and twenty people in a Bible College in England and foolishly I closed my eyes in prayer. We have got into a habit of doing that; they never did that in the Bible. They lifted their eyes up to heaven. I closed my eyes and more than one person told me afterwards that a tongue of fire sat on each head in that meeting, and they sent me an advertisement for a gas cooker with a ring of flames saying 'this is what it looked like' – and I missed it! Now when I am praying I tend to open my eyes to see what is happening.

Billy Graham was on his way to Scotland for his first crusade in Glasgow and he had been told that the Scots were a dour lot, having fed on porridge for years, and that they would not respond to his emotional appeal. So he and his fellow evangelists got into a railway carriage compartment, pulled the blinds down and got on their knees to pray about the Glasgow crusade, and Billy Graham records in his autobiography that 'the sound of a rushing, mighty wind' filled the railway compartment and they knew it was going to be alright.

When we are full, we overflow

But those are special things that don't occur regularly. But the *inside* – what happened to them on the inside – that is what we are concerned about, that is what we are going to ask about. Is it for you today? Well now, what happened on the inside? They were filled to overflowing with the Holy Spirit. Now let us just look at that. I stopped to get some petrol on the way to an event because I was running out. How do I know when the petrol tank is full? Well, we have the automatic pump now that shuts itself off, but we didn't used to have that. How did you know when your petrol tank was full? – when it overflowed out of the little hole at the back of your car. How do you know when anybody is full of anything? Well, God has provided you with an overflow. There is a little overflow in my bath at home. And I tend to do a lot of meditation in the bath. Do you? I really can. I am facing the right way, I relax. I have got a dish aerial around me to pick up messages from up there and I can get a whole book in a bath. I can stay there until the water is stone cold. (You see, it must be my theology – I've never been able to meditate in a shower, but when I'm immersed I can really meditate.) That's by the way – but there is an overflow just below the taps. There are two taps, then there is a hole, and if you get the bath full, there is a horrible noise of water being sucked out by that hole.

Now God provided every one of us with an overflow. It is about an inch and a quarter below our nose, so put your finger on your nose and just work down and you will find the overflow – and Jesus said that whatever your heart is full of will come out of your mouth. That is a sobering word. That is why more people have sinned with their mouth than any other part of their body. In fact, I heard of a vicar who told his congregation, 'I'm now going to show you that part of my body that brings me the most temptations', and there was a deadly hush and then he poked out his tongue! Well, whatever your heart is full of will come out of your mouth, said Jesus.

If you are full of fear, you cry out. If you are full of anger, where does it come out? If you are full of fun, where does it come out? You laugh! That is because you are filled with humour, filled with fun, and it comes out.

So, when you are full of the Holy Spirit, the sure and certain sign is something will come out of your mouth, and that is exactly what happened on the Day of Pentecost. They were all filled. Jesus had said: 'you will all be baptised in the Holy Spirit.' Now they were all filled – same thing – filled to overflowing and they began to praise. They burst into worship and praise exploded! The only thing was they were using languages they had never learned. I hate the English word 'tongues' as it sounds like uncontrolled babbling. 'Languages' is the word that is used here. They extolled the mighty works of God in languages they had never learned. But then, God knows all the languages, doesn't he? And somebody full of his Spirit can speak any language on Earth, and even any language in heaven – tongues of men or of angels.

So they exploded in praise to God in unknown languages. Of course a hundred and twenty people doing that make a big noise and everybody else in the temple heard it. They said they must be drunk. You don't behave like that in temples, just as people today say you don't behave like that in church. They said they were drunk and that was when Peter said, 'Drunk at nine o'clock in the morning? Unheard of! This is what Joel predicted.' This is the spirit of prophecy introducing the prophethood of all believers. That is what it was, and the spirit of prophecy was being poured out on all kinds of people, regardless of age, sex or class, as Joel had said. Age, sex or class doesn't matter here. The Holy Spirit is poured out on all flesh, all kinds of flesh.

Every year since, churches have celebrated and remembered that event because it was foundational to the Christian church, to all Christian living. So a hundred and twenty people knew what it meant to be baptised in the Holy Spirit. It was an experience, a conscious experience. They knew when it happened, they could date it. It happened on the Jewish Feast of Pentecost, the very Feast that remembered that God had sent the commandments through Moses on Sinai on that very day – not just ten commandments, but six hundred and thirteen of them. God had given his commandments and the immediate result at Sinai was that three thousand people died for breaking those commandments – that is in the book of Exodus.

The Spirit brings life

Three thousand died when the Law was given, but when the Spirit was given, three thousand were saved. That is why Paul later said, 'The letter kills but the Spirit gives life.' When churches are under rules and regulation and under letter, it kills. Legalism has killed more churches than license, but when the Spirit is there and the freedom of the Spirit – that is life! There are dead churches and there are live churches and the Spirit is what makes the difference. Not only did *they* know when it happened, everybody else present knew when it happened. That is the mark of later baptisms in the Spirit – not only do the people know but anybody around knows.

I was sitting in a public park in the town of Brasilia, the new capital of Brazil, with a lovely missionary, dedicated to his work. But he confessed sadly that he had never experienced supernatural power; he wistfully talked about the Holy Spirit who he didn't really know. He asked would I pray for him, and there in the public park with families picnicking all around I just laid a hand on him and said, 'Lord this dear man has served you so faithfully but all in his own strength. Please give him your power' – and he opened his mouth and shouted 'Hallelujah' at the top of his voice. He was filled to overflowing. All the families turned around and looked at him. I sort of shrank away from him, and then he looked at me and asked, 'Is that it?' I said, 'Well, it sounds like it to me.' I said, 'I'll bet you've never done that before in your life, especially in public; you're a real reserved Englishman.' I said he had never done such a thing before, but the proof of it was that within twenty-four hours he had healed two sick people which he had never done before. It was an explosion. He was filled to overflowing. That was all that came out but it was good enough for me because it was good enough for God. The man was full – to overflowing.

Well now, years later Peter didn't say we were baptised in the Holy Spirit or filled with the Holy Spirit. He simply said that's when we *received* the Holy Spirit. I want to make this quite clear. In your Bible, in mine, receiving the Holy Spirit, being baptised in the Holy Spirit, being filled with the Holy Spirit are all one and the same thing. And when Paul asked the disciples in Ephesus, 'Did you receive the Spirit when you believed in Jesus?' this is what he meant. When he wrote to Titus and said we have been justified by faith, saved through justification by faith and through the Spirit being poured out upon us copiously, that's what he meant. The language they used! They talked about the Spirit falling on us, poured out upon us, anointing us, filling us' – they exhausted the dictionary to try to describe this amazing experience. But it is all referring to one and the same – with one exception. There would be later occasions when they were filled but they didn't use the other language. They used 'anointed' for the one and only first pouring out. They used 'filled' for repeated experiences of being filled to overflowing. That's the only word used for later experiences of the Holy Spirit, and I believe we should stick to the way the Bible uses words.

So there it was. It was an event, but it was an event with effects. They were never the same again. There were five areas in their lives that were radically changed after the Day of Pentecost – after they had been baptised in the Spirit.

Five major effects of being filled with the Holy Spirit
Number one, they now had *confidence*. Time and again it says they were filled with the Spirit and spoke the Word of God *with boldness*, confidence. They were, first of all, confident in themselves. They had an assurance. Do you want

to be sure that God has forgiven you? Do you want to be sure you are a child of God? You won't get that assurance from scripture – too many Evangelicals try to. They say: 'Well, the Bible says so – I believe it – so it must be true.' That is a kind of mental deduction. The assurance that the New Testament talks about does not come from scripture but from the Spirit. The Spirit himself bears witness with our spirits that we are the children of God. John says: 'Hereby we know that we are children of God, because he has given us of his Spirit.' It is the Spirit's job to make you sure that you are a child of God and, sure enough, that is what happens.

After my wife was filled with the Spirit, I noticed the confidence that she had, boldness to speak, and it is not just assurance that you are right with God, it is a boldness in speaking to others. No shrinking, just: 'This is the truth'. We know it! And it gave them courage – the courage not only to live for Christ but to die for him. That takes confidence, doesn't it? It takes courage. That was the first area of their life that changed.

The second was that they now got *guidance*. They were *led* by the Spirit. The Spirit told them where to go, what to do. The Spirit took control of their lives and sometimes he forbade them to go where they were going. Other times he opened a door for them. You know, guidance is one of the biggest problems some Christians seem to have – trying to find out, trying to second guess God's mind. But the Spirit brings guidance. 'As many as are led by the Spirit of God, these are the sons of God.' It is the Spirit's job to help you to know the mind of Christ for your life, and the Spirit will lead.

Thirdly, they had *power*. They could do things they could never have done otherwise: supernatural power! They are called the gifts of the Spirit, and now they could do the things that Jesus had done. He had told them on the last night before he died: 'the works that I do, you will do too' – because the miracles that Jesus did were not done because he was the Son of God, they were done because he was the Son of Man working with the Holy Spirit. He never did a miracle until he was thirty years of age. He couldn't. He never actually preached until he was thirty years of age. He couldn't, because he was as real a human being as you and I are and therefore he was dependent on the Holy Spirit. He said, 'If I by the Spirit of God cast out demons then the kingdom of God has come upon you.'

Jesus never claimed credit for his miracles. He attributed them to the power of the Holy Spirit and that is why he was able to say: the things I have been doing you will be doing. Impossible? No, it's not! And that's why people who are baptised in the Spirit begin to see miracles happening.

The fourth thing they had after Pentecost was *unity*. They called it the fellowship of the Spirit; the Greek word '*koinonia*' is something much closer than having a cup of tea together. We had a church secretary who, every Sunday, used to say, 'Do come and have fellowship in a cup of tea with us afterwards.' And we had visions of all the church members piling into a big cup, having fellowship in a cup of tea! But, you know, that's not fellowship – that is just friendship. Fellowship is where you have something that joins you closely together. It was used of Siamese twins who shared the same bloodstream, and I have found this – people are talking about the unity in the church all over the place but it is never to be achieved by bringing us all into one denomination or one construction, organisation. Nor is it achieved by agreeing on all doctrine. Some people think that if you present each other with a list of your doctrines, you can say, 'If you agree with that, we can have fellowship.' That is not the way.

In the Bible, you have koinonia with everybody who has been filled with the Spirit – the same Spirit you have. And that is the first step toward doctrinal unity or organisational unity. Paul, in Ephesians 4, says: maintain the unity of the Spirit in the bond of peace *until we all attain to the unity of the faith*. It was a shock to me when I discovered Roman Catholics had been baptised in the Spirit. I thought: 'But I can't have fellowship with them, they teach this, this, this and this.' And I make it quite clear that I can't agree with all Catholic teaching – I don't. But I have found that I can have koinonia with Catholics who have received the Spirit. I think of dear Father Ian Pettit. He loved Jesus more than anyone I knew. I shared a bedroom with him at a conference and I said, 'Ian, I really hope that my room in heaven is next door to yours.' I never thought that I would ever say that to a Roman Catholic. But the unity *of the Spirit* comes first.

And when you meet somebody who has been filled with the same Spirit, you share the same bloodstream, you share the same air that you breathe, and you can have fellowship. That is the answer to the unity of the church: for us all to get filled with the Spirit. We can work out the doctrine later.

I was preaching to about sixty priests in a Roman Catholic seminary with a Cardinal sitting in the front row and they gave me my choice of titles so I chose as my title: 'What the Bible Doesn't Say about Mary'. Now that was sticking my neck out. But I did tell them what the Bible does say about Mary and I said, 'We Protestants are frightened to talk about Mary lest anybody think we are going Catholic.' I said 'you say too much and we say too little. Let us get back to what the Bible really says – for one thing she spoke in tongues.' That again caused a bit of a gasp, but you see there she is – I said: from the day she spoke in tongues she became an ordinary member of the congregation; her special job was finished. You see, I could talk like that because Ian Pettit himself came and wept on my shoulder afterwards. He said, 'For the first time I understand why you Protestants have problems about us Catholics.' You see, we were now able to maintain the unity of the Spirit *until we attained the unity of the faith*. And the early disciples had a unity – they had their disagreements but there was a unity there that they called the 'fellowship of the Spirit' – Siamese twins sharing the same source of life.

Finally, fifthly, they had *purity*. They now discovered they could live pure lives. They could be holy. They could live like God. They could now obey the command of both the Old and the New Testaments: 'Be holy, for I am holy,' says the Lord. They found they could do it. Now you try for the next week to live a holy life in your own strength – and you can come to confession then. Have you ever tried to live a holy life by yourself? You will never make it, and it is no good being told to do what you can – like the man sent to prison at seventy for 'life' and he said to the governor, 'I'll never make it', and the governor said, 'Never mind, just do what you can.' It is amazing how many people think that is what we are called to do to be holy – do what you can and God will forgive what you can't. But through the Holy Spirit they found they could live holy lives. They called it the fruit of the Spirit. They found that the Spirit could reproduce the character of Christ in them, they could become like Jesus.

The fruit of the Spirit
The fruit of the Spirit is only one fruit with nine flavours. You can't have any one of the flavours without the other eight. There is a fruit called Monstera Deliciosa. You take a bite and it tastes like an orange, you take another bite and it tastes

like grapefruit. It has the different flavours of fruit in one fruit, and the fruit of the Spirit has nine flavours – love, joy, peace, patience, kindness, goodness, faithfulness, meekness and self-control, and they are all descriptions of Jesus. The Holy Spirit, if you walk in the Spirit, will reproduce all those nine things. You can find some of them in unbelievers. You will never find all of them together in an unbeliever because only the Holy Spirit in a believer can produce all together. Love, joy, peace, patience, kindness, goodness, faithfulness, meekness and self-control – do you notice that the first three get you right with God, the next three get you right with everybody else, and the last three sort yourself out, so you get into good relationships with God, other people and yourself – through the Holy Spirit.

Now it is time to think about us today. I have been telling you about *there* and *then*, now it is *here* and *now*. We need to ask some big questions. Don't we need these very same five things? Would you not agree these are the greatest needs in the church today? These five effects (there are many more I could have mentioned) are urgently needed, but how are we going to get them? How can we have the effects without the event? That is the big question, or to put it differently, was Pentecost the first and last time it ever happened, or has it ever happened again? Could it happen now, or are we just every Whitsunday celebrating the birthday of the church that is now over? Are we just looking back to something rather than sharing in it?

Three current church views of the experience of Pentecost
Most churches on Whitsunday look back – they don't talk about having it now. They say: wasn't this a wonderful event that set the church going – full stop. Alas! Now I have entered into an area of controversy and I am going to be very honest with you and share that there are three major

different views on the question: 'Did Pentecost happen again?' They are very different views, and there are many churches among these different views. I am calling them the *Sacramental*, the *Evangelical* and the *Pentecostal*, and you must search the scriptures for yourself and come to one of these three views. Don't just listen to preachers and teachers or the denomination in which you were brought up, or your background. You must go to the Word of God and settle for yourself which of these views is correct.

The *Sacramental* view is very simple: Pentecost was never repeated, it was a one-off, unique event that got the church going; and that the Spirit was then given to the church to reside in the church, and if you want to benefit from that long-ago event, you simply do so by joining the church. You then 'enter in' to a community of the Spirit and the five effects will show in your life. Now, this view that the Holy Spirit now resides in the church provokes another question 'How do I avail myself of it as an individual?' – and the answer is: through the church's sacraments. The Catholic view of the Sacramental approach is that you receive the Holy Spirit when you are baptised as a baby, and that that is a double baptism – you are baptised in water and the Spirit at one and the same time. You won't remember either, but later in life you must believe that that is what happened and that is when you received the Spirit.

The Anglican version of it is that that is what happened in Confirmation and if you listen carefully to the Book of Common Prayer, you will realise that Anglicans are supposed to believe that in infant baptism or christening you are born of the Spirit, and in Confirmation you receive the Holy Spirit. And the bishop will actually say that to you when he lays his hands on you: 'Receive the Holy Spirit'. Nothing may happen, you may feel nothing – you probably will feel nothing – but you must believe that that is when you received. Quite frankly, I can't go along with that at all. It is as if I don't get baptised in the Spirit by Jesus, but by some priest. He is the one I need to go to. I believe that is totally contrary to scripture. Nobody other than Jesus can baptise you in the Holy Spirit, and he couldn't do it until he got back to heaven. But that is the belief.

Nearly two-thirds of the British population have been christened. Would you say that two-thirds of the British people have received the Holy Spirit? About a quarter of the population have been confirmed in their teens. Would you say that a quarter of our population have received the Holy Spirit? I just find the facts are right against this. My biggest problem is that I believe it is Jesus who does it, not a priest. But that is one view and probably the majority of church members in this country have been told that they have received the Spirit either in christening or confirmation, and even though nothing happened, you must believe it. I do know a bishop who was frightened out of his mind when he said, 'Receive the Holy Spirit' and the person did! They burst out in an unknown language and he nearly shot out of his robes! He had never seen it happen before. Well, it did happen on that one occasion (I know the bishop personally). But normally nothing happens and after all, if you were christened as an infant you have no recollection of it whatever and it probably means nothing to you, except a certificate with your name on it. That is one view and I am sorry if I seem a bit sarcastic but I just cannot line it up with the New Testament.

The second view you may be familiar with I call the *Evangelical* view, and I take a Bible teacher like John Stott as a representative of this view. It is that Pentecost was repeated but only three more times in the book of Acts – that it happened again with a bunch of Samaritans and it happened again with a number of Gentiles – Cornelius and his household – and that it happened again with John's disciples in Acts 19. But it has happened only four times in history and they call it the 'Pentecost of the Jews', the 'Pentecost of the Samaritans', the 'Pentecost of the Gentiles' and the 'Pentecost of John's disciples'. Therefore, they say don't expect Pentecost to happen to you. So how then do I tap into the Pentecost event? If the Sacramental view says take the sacraments of the church, the Evangelical view is: get converted – invite Jesus into your life and a whole lot of other euphemisms – make a commitment, make a decision, ask Jesus to take over. None of those phrases occurs in the Bible but we use them right, left and centre, and the teaching is that when you *received* Jesus as your Saviour and Lord *automatically* and usually *unconsciously* you received the Holy Spirit.

That is the most common view among Evangelicals and therefore you cannot use New Testament language about your conversion. Very few evangelicals talk of your conversion as being baptised in the Spirit. None of them use the word *filled* about your conversion. None of them talk about the Spirit being 'poured out upon you' or 'fallen upon you'. It becomes irrelevant language because how can you describe an unconscious experience with such powerful words? You can't, and so all those words used in the New Testament of being baptised in the Spirit are dropped in favour of these unscriptural terms like inviting Jesus into your life, etc. And above all, the New Testament does not talk about '*receiving Jesus*'! It did when he was on Earth because you could then invite him into your home – and it says that he came to his own people and his own received him not but as many as *received* (past tense) him (during the days of his flesh that is), to them he gave the authority to become sons of God who were born of God not of the will or flesh of man.

Repent, believe, receive

But that is all in the past tense – when he was on Earth; and he said then: 'If you receive me, you receive him who sent me', but after he ascended and the heavens received him from their sight, *never again* did the apostles talk of receiving Jesus. You can't receive him as he is no longer on Earth. He is at the right hand of the Father. What you *can* receive now and ought to be told to receive is the Holy Spirit who has taken his place on Earth. So they never preached to receive Jesus as your Lord and Saviour. They said: *believe in Jesus*, and *receive the Holy Spirit* – and they added one other thing before both. They said: *repent toward God*, believe in Jesus (at his right hand) and receive the Holy Spirit (now on Earth). So we have become all mixed up in our language and frankly it means that many, many Christians in this country don't know if they have received the Holy Spirit or not. There is no event they can point to, there is no Pentecost in their life when the Spirit was poured out upon them, when the Spirit fell upon them. Well, that is the second view and it was the second most common view in Britain. But I move on....The idea is that Pentecost died out after the apostles and such a view is often against prophecy and tongues today: that these things belong to the past.

So I come to the third major view which is now taking over the world church and is now becoming the major view in the twenty-first century – the *Pentecostal* view – and it starts with a very simple premise: Jesus is the same yesterday, today and forever, and therefore he is doing the same thing in the same way. It is a simple argument, and so this view expected every believer to have their own Pentecost, to tap into the historical event in an existential way. That sounds a bit complicated, doesn't it? Simply put, it is the same way that the apostles received the Spirit – and everybody else in the New Testament church. When you read the scripture carefully you find that the apostles expected every believer in the New Testament to have the same event in their lives. Peter said it again and again. He said, 'I couldn't help but accept Cornelius and his household because they received the Spirit just as we received the Spirit' – same experience, same event: filled to overflowing, sometimes in unknown languages, sometimes in their known language. Both happened in the New Testament – but an explosion through the mouth of words that came from God. That is what they looked for and they expected of every believer. That is why Peter and John rushed to Samaria because they hadn't had that there – they had repented, they had believed, they had been baptised, they were full of joy, but they hadn't had that. So Peter and John rushed down and they prayed for them and it says: 'as they prayed for each one, each one received his Pentecost'. It was the *normal* way that the Holy Spirit was received *then* – and Pentecostals believe *now*. Pentecost was only the *first* such occasion.

After all, John the Baptist had promised it to everybody he baptised in water. Did he add, 'Of course, it will only be for those of you who happen to be present on the Day of Pentecost'? It sounds ridiculous, doesn't it? No, he said that he baptised them in water but, 'Jesus will baptise you in the Holy Spirit.' It was promised to everybody, and on the Day of Pentecost Peter said, 'The promise is to you and to your children and to all that are afar off, as many as the Lord calls'. The promise of being baptised in the Holy Spirit is universal through time and space. You have already gathered that is my view. I was driven to it by a study of scripture.

David's testimony
Let me give you my testimony. I came to know Jesus when I was seventeen, through my cousin who was an evangelist

called Tom Rees in a place called Hildenburgh Hall. I didn't know the Holy Spirit. Through knowing Jesus I came to know the Father, and I knew Father and Son but if you had asked me if I knew the Holy Spirit I would not have quite known what to say. I certainly didn't know him to talk to, and so it was for years. When I was at Cambridge I did a postgraduate year when I could choose my study, and as one subject I chose 'What Happened on the Day of Pentecost in Acts 2?' – and I prepared a paper on it and my conclusion was very learned and, after quoting Greek and Hebrew scholars, I said 'nobody knows', and I finished up in complete ignorance. I thought it was too long ago and too far away for anybody today to understand what went on. I got a good mark for it, quoted the right scholars and threw in a bit of my own stuff.

Then I went into the ministry and I preached regularly but there was one day of the year I didn't like preaching on – Whitsunday, because I could no longer talk about the Father and the Son, I had to produce two sermons on the third person of the Trinity. I managed it out of books, but you know any discerning person would have realised I was just giving book learning like the scribes, whereas they recognised that Jesus knew what he was talking about, unlike the scribes. Well, it became a crisis. I decided like many preachers do (it is a naughty decision) to settle my doubt in the pulpit. A dear old lady said to her vicar, 'Please stop sharing your doubts with us. I've enough of my own.' But that is what we preachers sometimes do. So I announced that I would preach a series of twenty sermons on the Holy Spirit and I would take people through every reference to the Spirit in the Bible, from Generation to Revolution (Genesis to Revelation) all the way through, and I began the series.

I got on very well with the Old Testament. That was far enough away – I talked about the prophets being filled with the Spirit – Samson and all the others. And I got into the first three Gospels. That was okay. Then I got into John – chapters 14–16. I began to feel out of my depth and I had arranged to reach Acts 2 on Pentecost Sunday and I was now dreading it. I thought I had started and now I had to finish. I wondered what I would say on Whitsunday on Acts 2.

About that time, we had a man in the church who was the self-appointed leader of the opposition. I think there is one in most churches – do you know what I mean? Dear James, as his name was, or Jimmy, as everybody called him, was the self-appointed leader of the opposition, and in church meetings if I suggested something it was either, 'We've done it before and it didn't work,' or, 'We've not done it before and we're not changing.' I used to come back from a church meeting and I would say, 'Oh Jimmy, Jimmy.' And my wife would say, 'Don't worry about Jimmy. He's the only one opposing you and all the members are with you. Forget him.' I said I couldn't forget him. Well, I did get relief from him once a year. He had a weak chest and he would develop hay fever at the right time of year and then it would turn into lung congestion and he would be put to bed for up to six weeks and I have to say I rejoiced as we could be without Jimmy. Well, in this particular year it was when I was in the middle of these sermons on the Holy Spirit that he went down with it and was put to bed by the doctor for weeks.

I thought I should go to see him, as was the pastor's duty. So off I went to see him. He lay there, and as I went towards him I kept hearing in my brain: 'James 5, James 5, James 5'. I thought: well, he is James but what's the '5'? Then I remembered that James 5 says, 'Is any among you sick?' It goes on to say that the sick person should be anointed with oil and prayed for and the sick would be healed, and I thought, 'Oh no, Lord, you don't want me to do that for Jimmy?'

I got to him and there he lay, grey-faced, flat on his back, gasping for breath, and his first question was, 'What do you think about James 5?'

I answered, 'Well, I have been thinking about it. Why?'

He said, 'Because I'm due in Switzerland on Thursday on business and the doctor says I can't go, but would you come and anoint me with oil?' I said I would pray about it. That is a real get-out. It sounds so good! I went home and asked the Lord to tell me why I shouldn't do this – to give me a good reason why I shouldn't do it.

But on the Wednesday his wife rang me and asked: was I coming to anoint her husband? I agreed to go that night and I went to Boots the chemist and bought a big bottle of olive oil, and then I went into the church by myself and knelt in the pulpit to pray for him. Have you ever tried to pray for someone you are glad is sick? It really is a problem and I tried to pray and then suddenly I was praying for Jimmy with all my heart and soul. I really was, but not in English. It sounded like Chinese to me, and I finished that and looked at my watch. An hour had gone, just like that. I wondered if I could do that again. I bowed my head, thought of him, and I was praying in something like Russian. I thought, 'Oh boy! This is what happened in Acts 2! This is it! Wonderful things are going to happen tonight.'

So off I went with a few of the leaders and we got into his bedroom and we took James 5 and went through it just as if we were servicing a car. We said, 'Now the first thing is to confess your sins to one another.' So I turned to Jimmy and I said, 'Jimmy, I've never liked you' – that is confessing sins, you see. And he said, 'Well, that's mutual.' We went through it all and then I said, 'Right, now we anoint you,' and I took the cork out of the bottle and I poured it all over his hair – and guess what happened? Absolutely nothing! I got up and said, 'Well, we've done it all' – and I turned to run away. I ran as far as the bedroom door and I just turned back at the door and said, 'Have you still got your air ticket for tomorrow?' 'Yes, of course,' he replied. I said I would run him to the airport, and then I ran. The last thing I wanted to do the next morning was contact him so I didn't, but at ten o'clock the phone rang. 'Jimmy! Are you all right?' (Lack of faith!) He said, 'I'm fine. Can you pick me up at eleven?' I agreed and asked him if the doctor had said he could go. He said he had been to him and he had said he was clear. I asked him what had happened. He said in the middle of the night it was as if two giant hands squeezed his chest and he brought up two bucketfuls of liquid. He could breathe and he had been to have his hair cut, but the barber said he would have to shampoo him first as he had never seen such a greasy head of hair in his life.

Well, I ran him to the airport. Now I'll tell you three things. First, he became my best friend. Second, he and his wife got baptised in the Spirit. Third, he never had that problem again. That is not the work of the devil, is it? So there it was.

The next Sunday, I am in the pulpit again, taking John chapter 16 as my text. I gave the same sort of message as I had been giving for weeks and a young carpenter came to me afterwards and asked, 'What happened to you this week?' I said, 'Why, what do you mean?' He replied, 'You know what you're talking about now.' That young man is now a Baptist minister in Bristol.

Well, from then on I began to do things I had never done before in my life. The gifts became available. But look, I'm glad I was baptised in the Spirit without anybody else there because then I knew it was from him. People think that they must find somebody filled with the Spirit and then they will catch it from them. No! Nobody else can baptise you in the Spirit except Jesus. He is the first person to go to if you want to receive the Holy Spirit.

I was in Jerusalem some time ago. I was also in Gaza

actually, dodging missiles. But while I was in Jerusalem I bumped into Pastor Yun, the 'heavenly man' who wrote the book of that title. Every Christian needs to read that book. You will never grumble again after reading it. This man was tortured, suffered electric shocks, had his legs broken, yet walked out of prison as the doors opened in front of him – a man who went without food and water for 74 days, still alive and full of the Lord. But I had not read his book. I was ashamed to confess it to him when we met. We got on like a house on fire but I had never read his book. I have read it since. He wrote:

I wasn't sure who the Holy Spirit was. [He was a believer, had read his Bible, memorised it.] *I ran and asked my mother. She couldn't explain. She simply said 'I've already told you all I can remember. Why don't you pray and ask God for the Holy Spirit just like you prayed for your Bible.' My mother was illiterate so she had a shallow knowledge of the Bible. She had learned only to recite a few verses. This was a defining moment in my life. I had a desire for God's presence and power and now I realised how important it is to know God's written Word. I prayed to the Lord, 'I need the power of the Holy Spirit. I am willing to be your witness.' After the prayer God's Spirit of joy fell upon me. A deep revelation of God's love and presence flooded my being. I'd never enjoyed singing before but many new songs of worship flowed from my lips. They were words I had never learned before. Later, I wrote them down and these songs are still sung in the Chinese house churches to this day.* (Hattaway, Paul, *The Heavenly Man: The remarkable true story of Chinese Christian Brother Yun*, Lion Hudson, 2002, ISBN 978-1-854245-97-7.)

Songs he had never learned, words he had never learned, poured out. You notice the liquid language – 'flooded my soul', 'poured out', 'fallen upon'. That was his Pentecost. He immediately began to be led by the Holy Spirit – to be told where to go, who he would meet the next day, their names and even the clothes they were wearing so he would recognise them. He was living in the Spirit from then on and you must read his story.

What are the conditions for receiving the Holy Spirit?
I had to follow him in Jerusalem and speak after he had spoken to five thousand Christians from seventy-four countries, and I thought, 'Follow that?' So I just got up and said, 'Now you're going to hear from the "earthly man", that's me – he's the heavenly man.' Well, that was his testimony. So, finally, what are the conditions? What do you need to do to be ready to receive the Holy Spirit and be baptised in that wonderful Spirit?

First, there are *three basic steps* that I believe should be taken. *One, repent of all known sin and put right what can be put right; Two, believe in the Lord Jesus as your Saviour and Lord; Three, be baptised in water.* Those are the three basics. Then the next condition is very simple. Jesus said to ask, but he didn't say to ask once. *He said to go on asking and you will receive; go on knocking and you will have the door opened; go on. Go on asking.* People have said to me, 'You know, I once asked to receive the Holy Spirit and nothing happened.' You only asked once? Did you mean business? When my children wanted bikes: 'Daddy, can we have a bike?' 'Daddy, it will save bus fares.' 'Daddy, everybody else has bikes.' 'Daddy, Daddy, Daddy....' They don't ask once, they go on asking until they get.

We had some students in Guildford who shut themselves in a bedroom, locked the door and said, 'Lord, we're not leaving this room until you baptise us in your Holy Spirit.' By the next morning they came out changed. Do you really want this more than anything else? Then you will go on asking until you get. The context of that statement in

Luke chapter 11 is of the man who went on knocking at a neighbour's door until he got some bread for his visitors, and Jesus said that is how you are to pray. 'How much more will your heavenly Father give the Holy Spirit to those who go on asking him.' But I am going to add *three other conditions* which are necessary because of today's situation.

First, you need to study your Bible and search it, asking the Holy Spirit to guide you until you are absolutely convinced from the Word of God that this promise is for you and that Jesus wants to baptise you in the Holy Spirit. Don't just try it out, knowing that there are different views in the church. You must have your own conviction based on the Word of God. I am not interested in people wanting experiences for their own sake. Do you want the courage, the guidance, the power, the purity, the unity? Those are the reasons for asking for the Holy Spirit, not just to have a high. And expect to have happen what the Bible talks about. The Bible doesn't talk about laughing or dancing or falling on the ground. It talks about exploding through your mouth in praise to God. So you need to have your clear view before you ask. You are claiming a promise and if you are not sure what that promise is, you can hardly claim it.

Next, we are so full of *inhibitions and fears* today that you need to deal with them first. I have known people afraid of being a fool, afraid of what they might do when they hand control over to the Spirit, afraid of what people will say if they speak in tongues. I have known all kinds of inhibitions and fears, and particularly the British reserve. It is ten times easier to get somebody with a Spanish temperament to be filled with the Spirit than a reserved British person who has been controlling himself for so long that he is reluctant to let go.

Finally, in our situation, *we must be willing to be led by the Spirit afterwards*, whatever that leads to, whatever the cost or the consequence. A vicar came to me years ago and he asked me to pray for him to be filled with the Holy Spirit. I agreed on the condition that he, an Anglican vicar, would be willing to be baptised by immersion as a believer if the Holy Spirit told him to. He asked why I had asked him that. I said I was just trying to find out if he was willing to be led by the Spirit afterwards. He asked, 'Will the Holy Spirit tell me that?' I replied, 'He may or he may not. I think he's likely to, but what will you do if he does?' He said, 'Can I go away and think about it?' He came back three days later and he said, 'David, I've thought it through. I will do what the Spirit tells me, whatever it costs.' I prayed and he was filled and he went away and I didn't hear of him for twelve years, and then I saw a headline in a national newspaper: 'Vicar and entire church kicked out of the Church of England by Bishop', and it cost him his pension, his vicarage, his job. But he was obedient to the Holy Spirit.

Do you just want the experience of being baptised in the Spirit or do you want to walk in the Spirit afterwards, and be led by the Spirit? That is the big question.

Well, I have tried to teach you from the Word of God. I have shared my testimony. It won't be exactly the same for you, but the explosion of praise will. Now I must leave it with you.... and our Lord Jesus Christ.

ABOUT
DAVID
PAWSON

A speaker and author with uncompromising faithfulness to the Holy Scriptures, David brings clarity and a message of urgency to Christians to uncover hidden treasures in God's Word.

Born in England in 1930, David began his career with a degree in Agriculture from Durham University. When God intervened and called him to become a Minister, he completed an MA in Theology at Cambridge University and served as a Chaplain in the Royal Air Force for three years. He moved on to pastor several churches, including the Millmead Centre in Guildford, which became a model for many UK church leaders. In 1979, the Lord led him into an international ministry. His current itinerant ministry is predominantly to church leaders. David and his wife Enid currently reside in the county of Hampshire in the UK.

Over the years, he has written a large number of books, booklets, and daily reading notes. His extensive and very accessible overviews of the books of the Bible have been published and recorded in *Unlocking the Bible*. Millions of copies of his teachings have been distributed in more than 120 countries, providing a solid biblical foundation.

He is reputed to be the "most influential Western preacher in China" through the broadcast of his best-selling *Unlocking the Bible* series into every Chinese province by Good TV. In the UK, David's teachings are often broadcast on Revelation TV.

Countless believers worldwide have also benefited from his generous decision in 2011 to make available his extensive audio video teaching library free of charge at www.davidpawson.org and we have recently uploaded all of David's video to a dedicated channel on www.youtube.com

TAKE A LOOK AT YOUTUBE
www.youtube.com/user/DavidPawsonMinistry

THE EXPLAINING SERIES
BIBLICAL TRUTHS SIMPLY EXPLAINED

If you have been blessed reading this book, there
are more available in the series. Please register to
download more booklets for free by visiting
www.explainingbiblicaltruth.global

Other booklets in the *Explaining* series will include:
The Amazing Story of Jesus
The Resurrection: *The Heart of Christianity*
Studying the Bible
Being Anointed and Filled with the Holy Spirit
New Testament Baptism
How to study a book of the Bible: Jude
The Key Steps to Becoming a Christian
What the Bible says about Money
What the Bible says about Work
Grace – *Undeserved Favour, Irresistible Force
or Unconditional Forgiveness?*
Eternally secure? – *What the Bible says about being saved*
De-Greecing the Church – The impact of Greek thinking
on Christian beliefs
Three texts often taken out of context:
Expounding the truth and exposing error
The Trinity
The Truth about Christmas

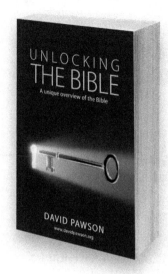

UNLOCKING THE BIBLE

A unique overview of both the Old and New Testaments, from internationally acclaimed evangelical speaker and author David Pawson. *Unlocking the Bible* opens up the Word of God in a fresh and powerful way. Avoiding the small detail of verse by verse studies, it sets out the epic story of God and his people in Israel. The culture, historical background and people are introduced and the teaching applied to the modern world. Eight volumes have been brought into one compact and easy to use guide to cover both the Old and New Testaments in one massive omnibus edition. *The Old Testament: The Maker's Instructions* (The five books of law); *A Land and A Kingdom* (Joshua, Judges, Ruth, 1&2 Samuel, 1&2 Kings); *Poems of Worship and Wisdom* (Psalms, Song of Solomon, Proverbs, Ecclesiastes, Job); *Decline and Fall of an Empire* (Isaiah, Jeremiah and other prophets); *The Struggle to Survive* (Chronicles and prophets of exile); *The New Testament: The Hinge of History* (Mathew, Mark, Luke, John and Acts); *The Thirteenth Apostle* (Paul and his letters); *Through Suffering to Glory* (Hebrews, the letters of James, Peter and Jude, the Book of Revelation). Already an international bestseller.

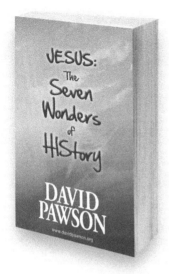

JESUS:
THE SEVEN
WONDERS
OF HISTORY

This book is the result of a lifetime of telling 'the greatest story ever told' around the world. David re-told it to many hundreds of young people in Kansas City, USA, who heard it with uninhibited enthusiasm, 'tweeting' on the internet about 'this cute old English gentleman' even while he was speaking.

Taking the middle section of the Apostles' Creed as a framework, David explains the fundamental facts about Jesus on which the Christian faith is based in a fresh and stimulating way. Both old and new Christians will benefit from this 'back to basics' call and find themselves falling in love with their Lord all over again.

OTHER TEACHINGS
BY DAVID PAWSON

For the most up to date list of David's Books
go to: **www.davidpawsonbooks.com**

To purchase David's Teachings
go to: **www.davidpawson.com**